I0484806

THREE "A"s FOR BUSINESS SUCCESS:

Attention & Retention Strategies

By Angela R. Edwards

#ThreeAsForSuccess

#AttentionAndRetention

Dedication

I dedicate *Three "A"s For Business Success: Attention & Retention Strategies* to my father, James Boyce, who passed away April 2014. "Daddy" was instrumental in helping me realize my dream of entrepreneurship – and he never ceased from telling me how proud he was to see me come into my own. I have no doubt that if he were here today, he would be overjoyed to know this book has come to fruition. Thank you, Daddy! I love and miss you still...

Daddy's Girl Always

Acknowledgements

I must first give honor and thanks to my Heavenly Father for endowing me with gifts so that I may help others. Without Him, I would not be able to compose and compile this publication to reach entrepreneurs and small business owners.

To my husband, James, daughter, Anequilla, son, Gerald, and granddaughters, Aniyah and Kelyce: Where would I be without you in my corner? I am thankful for your patience with me as I continually asked for [yelled about?] quiet time – and you granted me what I needed. I love all of you very much.

To my **TEAM** of insightful editors and supporters throughout the entirety of this project, I truly appreciate all of you. M.R. Scott of *M.R.S. Inspirations* has consistently taken me to task to continually improve upon the verbiage and potential issues with interpretation by the reader. Her guidance and advice have been stimulating [inspirational!], and I would not have produced my very best without her. Thank you, M.R. Scott, for making me step it up one line at a time! I love you always!

Secondly, M.E. Porter of *M.E. Porter Unlimited LLC* has been my business coach, accountability partner, and biggest cheerleader. When I had moments when I was too tired to write another word, she was right there – gently nudging me and reminding me of the end result: this book in YOUR hands, dear reader! Thank you, M.E. Porter, for being a friend first and for encouraging me along the way...ALL of the way! Love you, Murl!

Last but not least is my Ace-in-the-Hole: JDB Squire of *Glych in the System*. In the midst of all that was going on in his life on any given day, he stopped what he was doing to ensure that I remained authentic to my brand and my audience. There's something to be said about how music and words translate, and your musical talents have definitely shined through! Thank you, JDB Squire, for your intellect and time. I do not take them for granted. Much love to you today and always!

I did not want to forget one other person who believed in me and this project long before it came to realization: the first person to purchase my book, fellow Author L.A. Alicia. Thank you, my friend. I sincerely pray this book reaches deep within you much like yours did for me.

To the countless other enthusiasts who encouraged me along the way, you, too, are appreciated for your heartfelt congratulatory words and the smiles that kept me going.

About the Author

Greetings, Business Owner! Thank you for purchasing *Three "A"s For Business Success: Attention & Retention Strategies*!

I am Angela R. Edwards, Owner and CEO of Angela's Accurate Administrative Services (A.A.A.S.) – your one-stop source for online administrative support. My motto is, *"Let ME Put It Together...For YOU!"* Piece by piece, A.A.A.S. assists you in alleviating your workload, thereby ensuring you **SHINE** as you devote more valuable time to expanding your business.

In a nutshell, as a Virtual Assistant, A.A.A.S. provides administrative, technical, creative, and social media assistance to clients remotely from a home office. All services provided incorporate over 30 years of experience in government and private sector to include office management.

A big plus for YOU is that there are no overhead costs associated with contracting my services! You only pay for the service(s) rendered. As YOUR support, I work one-on-one with you to ensure your business continues to operate smoothly and efficiently. A *partial* list of tasks clients contract my services for include creating: Social Media Content, Newsletters, Brochures, Data Entry, and Email Management. A FREE 15-minute *"Put It Together Planning Session"* is available to new clients where you may find there are other duties not mentioned here that you perform but could be easily outsourced!

For example, a client needed a large multi-faceted project completed in short order. Rather than use a temporary service, she elected to contract with A.A.A.S. after the aforementioned FREE 15-minute *"Put It Together Planning Session"*. When the project was completed well in advance of the agreed upon deadline, her needs and expectations of an accurate and well-laid-out project were realized.

To paraphrase a quote from Winston Churchill: "You make a living by what you get; you make a life by what you give." I give ALL clients 100% - because 99.9% just won't do!

Moving forward, draw your attention to the three *"A"s* explored within this book: **Approachability**, **Adaptability**, and **Appreciation** – all of them equally important in the overall success of your business. Each will be explored in depth while providing guidance or, for some of the more "seasoned" business-owners, confirmation that your business is continuing to propel you to the next level.

So relax, enjoy a cup of coffee (or your favorite beverage), and delve into the three *"A"s*. We will then piece them together as you consider how to implement the strategies discussed.

Stay tuned for future book releases that are guaranteed to enrich other aspects of YOUR business' success!

Success Rests With A.A.A.S.!

Table of Contents

Chapter 1

Approachability

APPROACHABILITY
Avenues to Reach Target Clients

#ReachTargetClients

Approachability relates to your aptitude to reach out and connect with others by initiating interaction, making oneself available, and building relationships. With proper communication skills – such as listening, sharing, and taking the time to build rapport – people will gain a keen sense of how approachable you truly are.

Approachable Defined

The very definition of approachable clearly explains the key concepts that are imperative to your business' success. Dictionary.com simply states that someone who is approachable possesses the following characteristics: "...easy to meet, know, talk with..." For a brief moment, let's compare a few synonyms and antonyms for approachable:

Synonyms – Friendly. Sociable. Accommodating.

Antonyms – Unfriendly. Unsociable. Inaccessible.

We could go on and on, but I'm sure you get the gist of approachability's importance. Aren't those antonyms horrible words to associate with you and your business? Let's discuss how to be or remain (if applicable) approachable.

Step 1 of 3 – ASK YOURSELF: *AM I APPROACHABLE?*

Whether or not you are aware, people are always watching your interactions with others. I learned this lesson not too long ago when a customer of mine (obtained through a social media outlet) informed me that she had been watching me for quite some time before choosing my services. I was immediately flattered! At one point, however, I had to stop and question: "Was there anything I had done that was not consistent with my brand?" It was worth a trip back through my postings and ads to ensure that my message was, indeed, consistent. Phew! I caught a break! My messages relayed confidence, professionalism, and (most importantly) approachability – with a side of humor along the way. Those messages were a genuine reflection of who I am in both my business and personal relationships.

Think about the following attributes of your own personality when responding to this question: "*Am I approachable*?"

Do people tend to flock to you in social situations?

When you go shopping, are you the one who sparks up a conversation with a stranger while waiting in line?

In your business dealings, are you aggressive without being overly-assertive?

As a member of the audience during a presentation, would you sit up front with the potential that the presenter may single you out?

Are you oftentimes the first one to lend a helping hand, even when not asked to do so?

If you answered 'yes' to each of those questions, you are definitely on the right track. Give yourself a high-five! If you answered 'no' to at least one of them, let's work together to whip you into shape!

In some instances, you may be unaware of the reasons why you are perceived as unapproachable. One aspect to take into consideration is that your emotions are oftentimes influenced by the actions of others. What that means is this: You are generally introverted, which can be erroneously translated to mean you are shy, aloof, a loner, and lacking confidence. Let's face it: YOU are a business owner. YOU have taken the great leap to be independent. YOU are a star! *Shine*, my friend! *Shine* brightly for all to see!

There are positive and worthwhile effects associated with being approachable. When you can relay the message that you are open and friendly, people will quickly recognize those assets. Once those assets have been established, others may likely be more open to doing business with you. Your customers must be able to trust you. This is established by keeping your messages precise – no matter how they are transmitted – 100% of the time. Maintain the mindset that your business will not fail, which will keep you mindful that others' opinions of you truly do matter. Be sociable, friendly, and accessible. Once that type of message spreads about your business' reputation, your ability to succeed increases greatly!

Step 2 of 3 – ASK YOURSELF: *HOW DOES MY OUTWARD APPEARANCE CONVEY MY MESSAGE?*

Have you ever walked into a business and wondered if the employees ever smile or have a good day? The tension is overwhelming and rests heavily in the air during your transaction. You may even feel like running out the door and either returning another day or frequenting another establishment altogether. You would tell others about that unpleasant experience, correct? Imagine the uproar you could cause by the mere mention of that experience to even one person – who will tell another, who will then post it on all of their social media sites, and then...and then...and then. Before you know it, you have caused the establishment a hailstorm of negativity based on that one experience! That's obviously bad for business, right?

Let's flip it around now and look inward at you and the message your appearance conveys. What do you believe is one of the main characteristics that says "I'm approachable" when others first see you? Go on. Take a minute to think about it. I will wait... The answer is simple: your smile!

In a recent Harvard Business Review article, *The Science Behind the Smile*, Gilbert and Morse discussed the power of a smile and the effect it has on not only others, but ourselves as well. When we smile, we are more attractive to others and are apt to convey the message loud and clear: I am approachable! It is no secret that a smile represents joy. However, it may not be as obvious that a smile helps determine whether or not you are approachable. No matter how you are feeling at any given moment, your customers need to always feel that they are important and that you couldn't make it without them – which isn't far-fetched at all. You DO need them! "Never let them see you sweat." SMILE!

Step 3 of 3 – ASK YOURSELF: AM I NURTURING MY BUSINESS RELATIONSHIPS WITH MY CURRENT LEVEL OF APPROACHABILITY?

Earning a reputation as being approachable is not difficult; neither is it a walk in the park. For some, it comes naturally, while for others, it may take some hard work and dedication. The key here is to establish and nurture business relationships – whether in person, over the telephone, or via social media outlets. The networking opportunities that could blossom from genuine one-on-one interactions are endless! Following are a few helpful tips to follow:

Engage in an actual conversation. Sounds pretty basic, right? It might surprise you to learn that some people have not mastered the art of conversation, which has the potential to relay the message, "I do not want to be bothered" or "Not right now. I'm too busy to entertain you." OUCH! No Bueno! For starters, when you are approached and asked, "How are you doing today?" respond with more than, "I am fine. Thank you." A conversation would involve responding, returning the question, and then discussing an aspect of your life that would be of interest to the other party. In a business-setting, perhaps you could discuss a recent acquisition of a new product or customer. Anything is better than an awkward silence – and you never know: Your approachability factor may gain you someone new!

Give compliments. How does this factor into your approachability factor? By doing so, you can build your reputation as a pleasant person! Think about it: Who doesn't want to be around someone who can bring forth a smile? It must be noted here: To avoid potential deleterious misunderstandings, keep compliments focused on topics such as one's personality or a recent career highlight, while avoiding compliments that are not strictly related to the current business at hand.

Listen more than you speak. That seems self-explanatory, right? A large number of people are generally self-indulged. They love talking about themselves to anyone who will listen. Don't be that person. Remember: You have two ears and one mouth. Listen more than you speak. To prove yourself approachable, take a genuine interest in others. Chances are likely that an in-depth conversation will begin with you taking the first step. Inquire about a specific life event. Ask about their summer break. If you know the family well, ask how little Jimmy is doing at football camp. Indulge the customer in conversation that shows you care and have been paying attention. The customer will be truly appreciative of your efforts.

Include – not exclude. What does that mean? This is where your assertiveness as an approachable person comes into play. Invite others into conversations. If you see people standing off to the side, make an effort to draw them into the discussion. Don't assume that because they appear standoffish that they are. Be the go-getter that you already are and begin to build valuable relationships in the process!

Rudeness is an absolute no-no – and gossiping is even worse. If you want to witness your approachability factor plummeting to the deepest depths of the earth, participate in either of the aforementioned activities. Rude comments speak more about you than they do regarding the person or company you are referring to. Making rude comments says, "I am insecure. It makes me feel better to put others down." That is not the message you want to relay. In the same breath, spreading gossip is elementary and screams, "I spread others' secrets. I cannot be trusted with others' business." Keep your approachability factor high by keeping your comments positive and, when necessary, confidential!

Put It Together Step One

Do a self-assessment of your own approachability factor. Ensure you are making strides towards being more outgoing and personable with everyone you meet. Be friendly and wear your brightest, biggest smile. After all, your smile is your best asset! However, be cautious about having an over-the-top personality. Be genuine, open, and sincere. Nurture your business relationships by engaging in conversations, giving compliments, being a listener, including others, and avoiding rudeness and gossip. Within the realm of business, there is no opportunity to be lukewarm. Approachability requires that you be on fire to be a networking success!

Goal-Setting: Approachability Factors

Make the following commitments:

I am going to begin implementing the *Put It Together* strategies mentioned here in the following order within the following timeframes:

Ensure I am genuinely approachable to anyone and everyone.

Timeframe:

_____

Ensure my outer appearance and smile reflect my level of approachability.

Timeframe:

_____

Nurture my current and future business relationships to ensure continual growth opportunities.

Timeframe:

_____

Chapter 2

Adaptability

ADAPTABILITY
Meet Clients at their Needs and Be Flexible

#MeetClientsAtTheirNeeds

If I were to ask you, "What is one of the first animal species that comes to mind when you think of it being adaptable to its surroundings?" does the elusive, skillful chameleon make the list? Chameleons are known for changing their colors to adapt to their environment for the purposes of hiding from their predators and prey. Scientific studies conducted by National Geographic suggest that the chameleon changes in response to its mood, external temperature, and light. How's that for an adaptability factor?

Imagine applying the chameleon's adaptability to your business dealings. As part of the success that is made up of you and your unique style of managing your business, what instances come to mind when you've had to adapt in order to make a sale or provide a service? As you are thinking about your response, also consider how often you have had to acclimate in order to appeal to the needs of others.

Those questions may prompt you to respond with, "I'm 100% authentic with everyone under every circumstance." That may be your truth (and that is to be commended), but ponder over the following examples for just a moment:

During the course of any given day, you hold conversations with a variety of people. When you are at home, you speak with family members in a comfortable, casual manner. At work, you encounter employees and co-workers which cause your conversations to take on a more professional tone. While at work, you are accepting phone calls from other businesses and are confronted with a barrage of different personalities on each call – and you adapt. After work, you go on an outing with your friends and, again, your adaptability factor rises to the occasion.

In each instance mentioned, your communication style varied based on the other person's relationship to you. The *topic* of discussion is of little importance. You can talk about the weather and your speech will adapt to the *individual* to whom you are speaking; not the topic. You are mentally exhausted by the end of the day, but you do it all again the next day and the day after because you are passionate about success, right? (Say yes! Say yes!)

Other aspects that impact our communication include: one's age, profession, closeness of relationship, and culture. Each will have its own influence over your adaptability factor, and it pays to be aware of the impact each plays in your business.

Why Adaptation in Business is Imperative

Gone are the days when business was predictable. As a society, businesses used to be able to pre-determine gross yearly earnings by the end of the first quarter of the year because a trend had been set with customer spending. For example, I fondly recall working alongside my mother when she used to sell Christian literature. She would purchase a certain amount of books for the remainder of the year based on sales at the beginning of the year, their popularity, and a host of other factors. That information would be used to determine her year-end success – long before the final tally would be computed.

Today, it is not enough to be superb at one specific thing. As a business, you must be open to learning new things and how to do them **very** well. Competition is fierce! Finding ways to adapt to the needs of your customer base may actually take you out of your comfort zone. I once made a complex flowchart for a customer who needed to be able to convert it to a workable file on her website. I was able to complete the task with ease; however, after I had completed the chart, I was informed that the specific file type I had used to compose the chart was unable to be converted. Out of my comfort zone I went to ensure my customer's needs were met. I did some thorough research, found the perfect program to complete her project, and finished the task to perfection. Guess what I learned? *Success oftentimes rests on the other side of that untapped zone!*

Tackle Adaptation Expeditiously

Your business cannot afford to sit idly by and wait for you to raise your adaptability factor to an acceptable level. Because you are already in business, you must have adopted some traits that say to your customer base, "I am adaptable to your needs!" Hence, this next subject, while valuable to your overall success, may not come as a surprise.

The following are three significant areas that indicate you are a true go-getter – or are at least open to making some changes (if necessary):

You react positively to change. As I thought about this specific subject, I am mindful of the constant changes social media outlets put their users through. Algorithms, "pay-to-play", lack of public reach, and a host of other issues plague virtually every available resource in one way or another. Many people take issue with the consistency of changes and have the mindset: If it's not broke, why fix it? I say, "If it's not broke, improve on it!" (That's my governmental training kicking in.)

Many people easily adapt, recognizing that change is inevitable. After all, there is a bottom-line for those entities, too: making money. In business, we must accept that changes will occur – oftentimes outside of our reach. For example, costs for materials increase, suppliers go out of business, and customers want more bang for their buck. Remaining malleable versus bucking up against change will prove valuable in the greater scope of your business' bottom-line and will be reflective of your adaptability factor.

Stimulating personnel. A happy employee is a productive employee! Before I made the decision to become a business owner, I had my fair share of "productive employee" moments. Many are quite memorable. The common factor was that individuals in managerial positions acknowledged my hard work and rewarded me accordingly. Those rewards weren't always monetary. A simple "Atta girl" or the option to leave early from work one day went a long way, too. When you have employees who care about the company, why not go that extra step to ensure that when they go home they **desire** to return to work the next day? Do you see how your adaptability factor can increase a notch or two as you consider applying this principle to yourself and your employees? (Say yes! Say yes!)

Trial and error are your friends. I cannot stress the following enough: Revamp, revamp, and then revamp again! Consider for one moment how far cellular devices have come through the years. When phones were first installed in vehicles (Am I showing my age a bit?), their size and weight made it look like people were talking into a mini-fridge mounted on their shoulder – with buttons the size of pizzas! Over time, the phones became smaller in size with the added benefits of all that we have now: face-to-face chat (remember the cartoon _The Jetsons_?), mobile purchasing-power, speech- and touch-enabled activities, and much more!

Many people went through technological trial-and-error processes to get us to where we are today. Those individuals have a _very_ high adaptability factor – and I, for one, couldn't be more grateful. Imagine where we would be if the Wright Brothers had thrown in the towel after their first try at flying.

As this concept relates to your business directly, I recommend not becoming discouraged when one project, sale, or service doesn't skyrocket the way you envisioned. You may find that the new and improved process is far better than you had ever imagined – and your adaptability factor will soar!

What a segue for the final topic regarding adaptability!

Celebrate Failure!

Let's pause for just a moment to focus on failure. One of the reasons for failure is lack of adaptation. What I'm about to say may sound strange to some. I am hoping, however, that by the end of this section, your mindset will reflect the necessity to embrace failure as a *positive* experience. Keep an open mind, okay? Are you ready? Here it goes...

Businesses with a high adaptability factor celebrate failure! How abnormal is that? On the surface, it may seem peculiar – primarily because I cannot name one business that **wants** to have the label 'failure' attached to them. Dig deeper and you will see that failure allows for reflection on what went wrong and how the process/product/service can either be improved upon or eliminated altogether.

Relate the experience to an experiment. Remember those fun times in Science class with the beakers and the flame? All of those fun colors resulting from mixing two or more chemicals together? What you learned along the way were new and improved processes that became simpler as time progressed. As the old adage says, "If at first you don't succeed, try, try again!"

Do you now see the relevance of why I encouraged you to keep an open mind?

Put It Together Step Two

Much like the chameleon, adaptation is a constant process. You and your business are unique – and it does not matter if you fall under an umbrella company. The manner in which **you** handle your business is your distinctive style, and you should take great pride that you are where you are today. Remain focused on the future. Today's small success could be tomorrow's next big leap! Always be open to change because in business, there are no constants. Even the biggest companies recognize the need to be aware of their competitors' inner-workings and adapt to *exceed* customer expectation. Rise to the occasion at every turn, my friend! Keep an open mind and be willing to meet your customers' needs as they arise. This can only be accomplished if you are aware of all of the factors that make up your business. If you have personnel, ensure that you are bringing out the best in them by making them feel they are more than 'just an employee'. Take the time to foster their growth – and keep them happy! Remember that trial and error are critical aspects of growth. Become encouraged when things do not work out as planned; it may prove to be an opportunity to progress to the next level in your business! It's all a process, and your adaptability factor will reflect your desire to be a success. Others will see it in you, too!

Goal-Setting: Adaptability Factors

Make the following commitments:

I am going to begin implementing the *Put It Together* strategies mentioned here in the following order within the following timeframes:

I will become more aware of my adaptation principles when speaking with others.

Timeframe:

_____

I will have a positive reaction to change, realizing that nothing is constant.

Timeframe:

_____

I will begin to celebrate failures and recognize that they are opportunities for change or improvement.

Timeframe:

_____

Chapter 3

Appreciation

APPRECIATION
Have an Attitude of Gratitude

#AttitudeOfGratitude

"Gratitude is not only the greatest of virtues, but the parent of all others." M.T. Cicero

There was a time when customer appreciation was at the forefront of a business' success. Prioritizing customer retention and win-back programs should be at the top of your list. When businesses understand that customers should be acknowledged, recognized for their patronage, and thanked, retention numbers will begin to increase. Your profits will grow simply because you are an appreciative business owner!

Appreciation seems to be a lost art in many aspects of modern society. Simple phrases like, "Thank you", have been hidden deep in the English language and oftentimes surface only when there is a *mutual* exchange of gratitude between parties. Appreciation and communication go hand-in-hand. **One way to communicate your feelings is to extend genuine thanks**.

Imagine for just a moment...

A common negative scenario you may be able to relate to on some level as it relates to appreciation (or a lack of) could be the following:

As you are exiting a store, you hold the door open for the person entering. Appreciation (and manners) would warrant that you can expect a "Thank you" that sometimes never comes. How rude of that person not to acknowledge your act of kindness!

Can you relate? Has that ever been you? That one rude individual can leave you feeling as if you will never hold a door for another person a day in your life. That feeling of 'payback' is an unfair but justifiable thought because it is part of the human condition to feel that way. However, be sure not to follow through with negative behaviors in the future in like instances.

Big Business' Big News

Why is it big news when big businesses show appreciation to their customers? The answer is simple: It's not often enough that the customer is acknowledged outside of a 'thank you' on the bottom of a receipt. Just think: When was the last time a company president or high-level executive personally reached out and thanked you for your patronage? A simple note of gratitude would surely signify appreciation, right?

In business, showing customers appreciation is imperative in order to reach your highest level of success. Remember this: Were it not for your customers, you would not have a business to operate! The most difficult aspect of customer appreciation is deciding which avenue would retain and keep them coming back for more. There are no clear-cut ways to appeal to your ideal customer. It would benefit you, Mr. /Ms. Business Owner, to determine your customers' needs and establish an appreciation program based on your findings. Ask questions. Allow your customer to openly discuss what they would like in return for their continued business. Ensure they know they are part of the process.

Technology's Impact on Extending Appreciation

Technology has become a double-edged sword: Excellent for ease of reach to our ideal customer while at the same time, it is the leading cause of the downfall of communication in general. As a society, we have been rewired to believe that an email is the equivalent of a hand-written letter. Our wireless devices provide texting services that have taken the place of phone calls to relay messages. In the midst of it all, the level of appreciation from days of old has drastically decreased and is suffering at the hands of our technological advances. It would appear the basics of human interaction have been forgotten.

The Secret Weapon

As part of the corporate culture, the "secret weapon" that can propel your business past your competitors is appreciation. It is not enough to have customer satisfaction. A customer can be 100% satisfied and never return or utilize your services again. Your business operates on repeat customers, customer retention, **and** customer loyalty. You must create a culture of appreciation to ensure your customers will not only return, but also speak highly of you to others about the services/products you provide. There are no smoke-and-mirror effects permitted in the process. You should make your intentions clear and be genuine or else your efforts will be for naught.

What to Say?

Words of appreciation do not have to be listless and common. When your words are sincere, they will be able to flow freely. Henry Clay is quoted as once saying, "Courtesies of a small and trivial character are the ones which strike deepest in the grateful and appreciating heart." Whatever message you choose to convey, say it with a smile – no matter the forum by which it is relayed.

What to Do?

What can be done to ensure your customers are feeling appreciated? Some options include:

Creating and launching a "Thank You" video campaign to be shared on YouTube and/or your website. With it, you can personally (and individually) thank your customers by mentioning their names and the product or service associated with them. This affords you the opportunity to show appreciation while also advertising!

Dedicating a special Customer Appreciation Day just for them. On whatever day you choose, offer a significant discount on your products or services (for example) – for that one day only. Advertise well in advance of the event. Contact your customers via email or whatever means you have available. Make it a grand affair! I can assure you, as a recipient of this type of offer, I truly felt appreciated – as will your customer base.

Giving away freebies. Who doesn't love and appreciate free stuff? Try hosting an online contest with all of the bells and whistles. Perhaps you have a new product you are going to spotlight soon and you want to share it with one lucky winner. This avenue can boost engagement among current customers and likely draw in new ones! The possibilities are endless. Be creative, but ensure the offer remains directly related to your business venture.

Whatever option you choose, make sure showing your customers appreciation is not a one-time event. Your customers will come to expect the same treatment again and again – as they should. Imagine the positive chatter about your business, Mr. / Ms. Business Owner! Word of mouth can either make or break your company. Don't be on the 'potty-mouth' end of your customers' conversations. Be appreciative!

Put It Together Step Three

Showing appreciation is not an option; it's a necessity. Your business' current and future successes rest with your ability to not only *gain* but also *retain* happy customers. This can be accomplished by ensuring the customer is part of the process by which you determine the avenue to show appreciation for them. While technological advances have proven to make communication much swifter than the days of old, they have also made for relationship-hindrances. Make a conscious effort to rise above the expectations of your customers that they will **not** receive acknowledgment for their patronage. Reach out to connect with your customer base by appreciating them openly, genuinely, and often. Your customers will, in turn, grow to appreciate you and likely recommend your products or services. Remember: Say it with a smile! No matter the avenue you choose, ensure your customers are made to feel they are a critical aspect of your success. After all, aren't they?

Goal-Setting: Appreciation Factors

Make the following commitments:

I am going to begin implementing the *Put It Together* strategies mentioned here in the following order within the following timeframes:

I will be mindful that my customer base is the reason I am a successful business owner.

Timeframe: _____

I will devise ways in which to acknowledge customer loyalty.

Timeframe: _____

I will ensure my appreciation techniques are personalized.

Timeframe: _____

CONCLUSION

Fellow business owner, you have reached the end of *Three "A"s for Business Success: Attention & Retention Strategies*! Thank you for investing your valuable time to read this publication. It is my sincere hope that there was something new that you can and will apply to your everyday business dealings that will propel your business to the next level. I am excited for you and the endless possibilities as you begin to implement the strategies listed.

All throughout this book, you have been encouraged to think not only outside-of-the-box, but to also create your own ways in which to be a success – ways in which you may not have previously considered. With the ever-changing atmosphere in today's competitive business world, you must remain in tune with the business environment and your employees' level of happiness. Focusing energies on customers' needs and retention is paramount. You need them more than they need you, and they must be made to feel they are number one in your business. You, my friend, are limitless! Begin to embrace and believe in the possibilities ahead of you. The world is waiting for you to **SHINE** and needs what **you** have to offer.

I wish you the greatest of success. Be well today and always!

Angela R. Edwards, Author

CONTACT and CONNECT with
AUTHOR ANGELA R. EDWARDS

I can be reached via the following avenues:

Web: www.AngAccAdminSvcs.com

Email: info@AngAccAdminSvcs.com

Phone: (832) 819-3970

 http://bit.ly/AAASLinkedIn

 http://bit.ly/AAASFBook

 http://bit.ly/AAASTwitter

 http://bit.ly/AAASInsta

 http://bit.ly/AAASPinterest

 http://bit.ly/AAASYouTube

 http://bit.ly/AAASGoogle

I make every effort to connect with my fans and followers. When you reach out via the aforementioned avenues, please state that you are coming from *Three "A"s For Success*. As well, your feedback on GoodReads regarding this reading experience would be greatly appreciated.

SOURCES

Approachable, Dictionary.com Unabridged, Retrieved November 3, 2014.

Daniel Gilbert and Gardiner Morse, The Science Behind the Smile (Harvard Business Review, 2012).

Henry Clay,(n.d.) Quotable Quotes (GoodReads).

Marcus Tullius Cicero, Selected Works (Penguin Classics, 1st Edition, 1960).

National Geographic, (1996) Meller's Chameleon: Chamaeleo Melleri, Retrieved November 3, 2014.

Peter Drucker, Innovation and Entrepreneurship (Routledge, United Kingdom, 2007).

Winston Churchill, (n.d.) Quote by Winston Churchill, Retrieved November 3, 2014.